PIANO SOLO

HYMN SOLOS
FOR
WORSHIP

ARRANGED BY VICKI TUCKER COURTNEY

ISBN 978-1-4803-4234-7

HAL•LEONARD®
CORPORATION

7777 W. BLUEMOUND RD. P.O. BOX 13819 MILWAUKEE, WI 53213

In Australia Contact:
Hal Leonard Australia Pty. Ltd.
4 Lentara Court
Cheltenham, Victoria, 3192 Australia
Email: ausadmin@halleonard.com.au

Visit Hal Leonard Online at
www.halleonard.com

BLESSED BE THE NAME
(with "Praise Him! Praise Him!")

Words by WILLIAM H. CLARK (verses)
and RALPH E. HUDSON (refrain)
Traditional Melody
Arranged by Vicki Tucker Courtney

Joyfully (♩ = 112)

PRAISE HIM! PRAISE HIM!
Words by FANNY J. CROSBY
Music by CHESTER G. ALLEN

BLESSED BE THE NAME

CLOSE TO THEE

Words by FANNY J. CROSBY
Music by SILAS J. VAIL
Arranged by Vicki Tucker Courtney

HE'S GOT THE WHOLE WORLD
IN HIS HANDS

Traditional Spiritual
Arranged by Vicki Tucker Courtney

Triumphantly (♩ = 112)

HIGHER GROUND

Words by JOHNSON OATMAN, JR.
Music by CHARLES H. GABRIEL
Arranged by Vicki Tucker Courtney

I AM HIS AND HE IS MINE

Words by GEORGE W. ROBINSON
Music by JAMES MOUNTAIN
Arranged by Vicki Tucker Courtney

JESUS, LOVER OF MY SOUL

Words by CHARLES WESLEY
Music by JOSEPH PARRY
Arranged by Vicki Tucker Courtney

LEANING ON THE EVERLASTING ARMS

Words by ELISHA A. HOFFMAN
Music by ANTHONY J. SHOWALTER
Arranged by Vicki Tucker Courtney

Joyfully (♩ = 126)

O LOVE THAT WILT NOT LET ME GO

Words by GEORGE MATHESON
Music by ALBERT LISTER PEACE
Arranged by Vicki Tucker Courtney

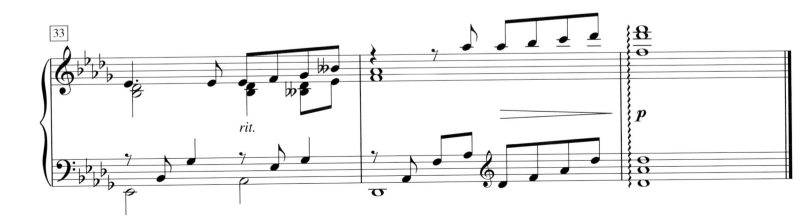

ROCK OF AGES

Words by AUGUSTUS M. TOPLADY
V. 1,2,4 altered by THOMAS COTTERILL
Music by THOMAS HASTINGS
Arranged by Vicki Tucker Courtney

TAKE MY LIFE AND LET IT BE

Words by FRANCES R. HAVERGAL
Music by HENRI A. CÉSAR MALAN
Arranged by Vicki Tucker Courtney

Simply (♪ = 133)